SCHOLASTIC

EASY SIMULATIONS

Explorers

by Tim Bailey

New York • Toronto • London • Auckland • Sydney
Mexico City • New Delhi • Hong Kong • Buenos Aires

Teaching
Resources

Dedication
To my parents, Ken and Judy, and to my sister, Stacie

Acknowledgments
To Maria Chang and all of my friends at Scholastic. You're the best!

Editor: Maria L. Chang
Cover design by Jason Robinson
Cover illustrations by Doug Knutson
Interior illustrations by Doug Knutson and Maxie Chambliss
Interior design by Holly Grundon

ISBN-13: 978-0-439-57815-8
ISBN-10: 0-439-57815-9
Copyright © 2008 by Tim Bailey
All rights reserved.
Printed in the U.S.A.

3 4 5 6 7 8 9 10 40 18 17 16 15

Contents

Introduction

August 26, 1495

" . . . suddenly a terrible storm is at our ship. Huge

waves are crashing on the deck and the wind is ripping

our sails. It came so suddenly we were not ready . . . "

This quote is taken, not from the log of a sailor in the late 15th century, but from the journal of Manuel, a fifth-grade student in my class who was role-playing a ship's steward on board a ship named *The Spanish Explorer* during our weeklong simulation. Using simulations in the classroom is one of the most powerful teaching methods you can choose. Students learn most when they see a purpose to an activity, are engaged in the learning process, and are having fun. Children love to role-play, and they do it naturally. How often have you overheard them say something like, "Okay, you be the bad guy, and I'll be the good guy"? Why not tap into students' imaginations and creativity and teach them by engaging them in a simulation?

What Is a Simulation?

A simulation is a teacher-directed, student-driven activity that provides lifelike problem-solving experiences through role-playing or reenacting. Simulations use an incredible range of effective teaching strategies. The simulation in this book, in particular, addresses a variety of academic content areas and fully integrates them into a single, weeklong social studies activity. Students will acquire a rich and deep understanding of history that would be impossible to gain through the use of any textbook. They will take responsibility for their own learning, discover that they must work cooperatively with their team in order to succeed, and apply skills in logic to solve the problems that they encounter. You'll find that *all* of your students will be motivated to participate in this simulation because they will be fully supported by their teammates and by you. Manuel, in the example above, is new to this country and speaks little English, but with the help of his team he was able to understand, participate, and contribute as much as any other student in the class. At the end of his journal, Manuel wrote in Spanish, "I liked this very much. I got to be a sailor and explore a new place. It was fun."

History Comes Alive

Easy Simulations: Explorers is designed to teach students about the Age of Discovery by inviting them to relive a part of this critical period in history. Over the course of five days, they will re-create some of the experiences of those brave individuals who opened the door to the "new world." By taking the perspective of a historical character living through this period, students will see that history is so much more than just names, dates, and places, but rather real experiences of people like themselves.

Students work together in groups and use their problem-solving skills to deal with the challenges of sailing from the ports of the "old world" in Europe to the shores of the "new world" in the Americas. Throughout the simulation, they will keep a log of their experiences. At the end of the simulation, they will write a letter to the monarch who provided them with their royal charter, describing what they have experienced and what they have learned from the activity. You can use both students' personal logs and letters as assessment tools to determine how much they understand and appreciate what it was like to be an explorer in Christopher Columbus's time.

Everything You Need

This book provides an easy-to-use guide for running this five-day simulation—everything you need to create an educational experience that your students will talk about for a very long time. You will find background information for both you and your students, describing the history of explorers during the Age of Discovery. You'll also find authentic accounts—from logs and journals written by people in the late 15th and early 16th centuries who experienced the same trials that your students will be enduring—as well as a map, tables, illustrations, and reproducible student journal pages. There are even directions for making and using some authentic navigational tools at the end of the book.

Before you begin the simulation, be certain to read through the entire book so you can familiarize yourself with how a simulation works and prepare any materials that you may need. Feel free to supplement with photos, illustrations, video, music, and any other details that will enhance the experience for you and your students. Enjoy!

The Age of Discovery

Columbus

October 12, 1492 – When Christopher Columbus set foot on the island of San Salvador in the Caribbean, little did anyone suspect how much his "discovery" would impact history. The fact is Columbus did not discover America. People have inhabited the Americas for thousands of years before Columbus arrived. Columbus was not even the first European to reach the Americas. That distinction probably belongs to the Vikings, who beat Columbus to America by 500 years. However, it wasn't until after Columbus arrived in the Americas—and returned home to tell about it—that the world changed forever.

The historical events that led to Columbus's arrival in the Americas date back two hundred years before his voyage. When Marco Polo returned from China in 1295, after spending several years in the court of the Chinese Emperor Kublai Khan, he wrote a book called *The Description of the World*. In this book Marco Polo told of the many wonders and the great wealth of China. However, it wasn't until the mid- to late 1300s, when a renaissance began in Europe, that trade routes were finally opened with the Songhai Empire in North Africa, and brisk trade started between Europe and China through the famous Silk Road. Yet Europeans were not happy with this trade arrangement. China had all the advantages in this partnership, and the Europeans wished to find a better, more economical way to get to the rich markets of Asia. So for the next two hundred years, until Ferdinand Magellan successfully circumnavigated the globe in 1522, much of Europe embarked on an "Age of Discovery" and explored the world not only for trade but also in the names of religion and curiosity.

Easy Simulations: Explorers © 2008 by Tim Bailey, Scholastic Teaching Resources

THE AGE OF DISCOVERY (CONTINUED)

Exploration has always been the realm of visionaries, and one of the most important visionaries in the history of exploration was Prince Henry of Portugal. He organized a school of navigation to train sailors to be explorers and developed a new style of ship that made longer sea voyages possible. He then sent expeditions south to find a way to sail around the continent of Africa and on to Asia. His first expeditions set out in 1419. Prince Henry's dream of having a Portuguese ship sail around Africa to Asia became a reality when Vasco da Gama sailed around the Cape of Good Hope and reached India in 1498.

While other explorers focused on getting around Africa to reach Asia, Italian sailor Christopher Columbus had a brainstorm—sail west across the Atlantic Ocean to reach the east coast of China! Unfortunately, his idea was based on a false premise. He believed that the distance from Europe west to China was some 3,000 miles. In reality, it is about 10,000 miles with two then-unknown continents in the way.

In order to get the financial backing he needed to try out his theory, Columbus had to be very persistent. He went to the King of Portugal with his plan, but Portugal was already investing its money in an attempt to sail around Africa. Undeterred, Columbus went to Spain's King Ferdinand and Queen Isabella in 1486 with his idea. But they turned him down. For six years, Columbus kept returning to the Spanish court and presenting his case for sailing west to China. Finally, for both religious and economic reasons, Queen Isabella relented and granted Columbus a royal charter, which gave him two ships and the funds to hire a crew and obtain supplies. Columbus bought two more ships (one turned out to be not seaworthy), hired 90 sailors, and prepared his expedition. On August 3, 1492, Columbus sailed from Palo, Spain, aboard his flagship *Santa Maria*, along with the *Pinta*, and *Santa Clara* (nicknamed *Niña* by the crew) across the Atlantic Ocean—and into history.

After Columbus's unwitting "discovery," Portugal, England, France, and other countries joined Spain in a quest to explore and exploit the Americas. They took home gold and silver, many new plants and animals, as well as slaves. In turn, they brought horses, wheat, and other kinds of flora and fauna unknown in the Americas, as well as disease and death.

Organizing and Managing the Simulation

Before students embark on their five-day journey, you will need to set the stage for the simulation. First, make photocopies of the reproducible pages at the end of this section:

- The Life of an Explorer (pages 18–19)

- Choose a Role (page 20)

- Personal Log (pages 21–22)

- Ship's Log (page 23)

- Royal Charter of Spain (page 24)

- Royal Charter of Portugal (page 25)

- Ship's Supplies Table (page 26)

- Disease Table (page 27)

- Navigation Table (page 28)

- Crew Morale Table (page 29)

- Ship's Mishap Table (page 30)

- Rubrics (page 31)

- Simulation Spinner (page 32)

Explain to students that they will be re-creating history, using the simulation and their imaginations to experience what it was like to be an explorer in the late 15th century. They will be taking on the roles of various explorers in that period and face the same situations that those people faced.

Distribute copies of "The Life of an Explorer" to students. You might also want to reproduce the pages on transparencies to display on an overhead projector. Read the selection together to build students' background knowledge about the period they're going to live through. Then divide the class into groups of four or five students. These student groups will be working together throughout the simulation, so members will need to be seated together during the activity. Explain that the decisions they make within their groups will determine whether they find fame and fortune or an early watery grave.

Choosing a Role

After you have divided the class into small groups, distribute the "Choose a Role" handout, which describes the various roles students can play during the simulation. Invite students to select a role from the handout, explaining that these roles were typically found in explorers' ships sailing in the Age of Discovery. Each role comes with its own set of special skills, with strengths and weaknesses indicated by a number ranging from 1 to 5. These numbers are called "attributes." The higher the attribute number, the more able the character. (See Attributes, below.) Students should pay special attention to their Health attribute. The Health number shows how healthy a person is—5 is perfect health, and 0 is dead. This number can change throughout the simulation.

Encourage students within each group to choose a variety of roles to make the simulation more interesting. While any combination of roles is possible within each group, it may not be wise to have a group of, say, five surgeons in a ship's crew.

Attributes

Attributes are the numbers that make each explorer role unique. The attributes are Strength, Common Sense, Seamanship, Negotiation Skill, Medical Expertise, and Health. Throughout the simulation, attribute numbers will be used during "skill spins" to resolve various situations that the explorers will encounter. Students spin the spinner (or roll a number cube) and compare the number they spun to their attribute number to determine whether their attempt at solving a problem is successful or not.

For example, say a broken mast has fallen across a crew member in the simulation. In order to move the mast, one of the explorers (a student) must make a spin and compare that number to her Strength attribute. If the number she spins is equal to or lower than her Strength attribute, she has succeeded in moving the mast. If the number spun is higher than her Strength attribute, her Strength was insufficient, and she has failed. Each explorer is allowed only one skill spin per situation. In other words, if a student fails in her Strength spin, she cannot attempt to move the mast again. Someone else in the group would have to try his luck by making another Strength spin.

Below is a description of the various attributes:

Strength: The physical strength and stamina of a person. This determines how easily an explorer can perform tasks that require physical power.

Common Sense: A person's wisdom and ability to understand and deal with difficult situations.

Seamanship: A person's experience on the sea and his knowledge of what it takes to be a good sailor.

Negotiation Skill: How well a person can reason with or influence other people.

Medical Expertise: How skilled a person is at caring for the sick and injured and handling medical emergencies.

Health: A person's current health. All explorers start with a Health of 5. During the simulation an explorer might lose a Health point due to sickness, injury, or starvation. If the Health number falls to 0, that explorer has died. The only way to regain lost Health points is to have someone on board the ship make a successful Medical Expertise spin. Each scenario describes when a Medical Expertise skill spin may be made. If an explorer dies at some point during the simulation, that student should still participate in group decisions and discussions as the "unseen conscience" of the ship's crew. The student should still be expected to keep up his or her personal log.

Keeping a Personal Log

After students have chosen their roles, distribute copies of the Personal Log pages—one copy of the cover page and five copies of the blank log entry page. Explain to students that they will be recording their experiences during the simulation in their personal logs on a daily basis. To give the logs a more realistic look, have students make a cover using a sheet of 12-by-18-inch brown construction paper or a large brown paper grocery bag. Demonstrate how to "sew" the diary pages inside the cover page using a hole punch and yarn, as shown.

On the cover page, have students fill in the information about the character they've chosen—the name, role, and attribute numbers. When writing in their personal log, have students record the date of the simulation, not the actual date. For example, use December 9, 1495, rather than May 9, 2009. Students should record the events in that day's episode. Encourage them to write their log entry "in character," as if the events had really happened to them. This activity gives students the opportunity to take on another person's perspective and to experience history "firsthand."

A student's log often yields rich insights into the student's understanding of historical events and how they impacted ordinary people's lives. Use these logs as your primary tool for assessing students' participation and evaluating how well they understand the simulation's content. (See Assessing and Evaluating, page 16.)

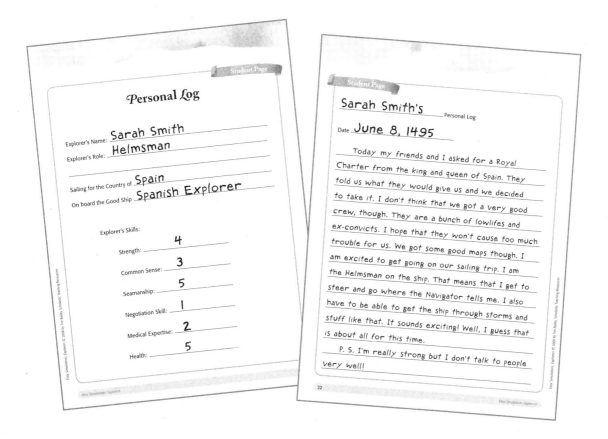

In addition to their personal logs, each explorer group will also keep a Ship's Log. Encourage each group to decide upon a name for their ship, such as *Spanish Explorer*, and record it on the Ship's Log. Students should also record the names and roles of each member and track the crew's Morale. This number reflects the attitude of the crew and will be adjusted up or down as events occur during the simulation. If this number ever drops to 0, the explorers must immediately spin on the Crew Morale Table (page 29).

The Royal Charter

Many explorations in the 15th and 16th centuries were made possible by the aid of a *royal charter*—a contract between an explorer and a king or queen. This agreement provided an explorer with a ship, crew, maps, and supplies in exchange for a country's claim to any lands that the explorer might discover as well as a share in any profits made by the expedition. Christopher Columbus, for instance, demanded that he be named Admiral of the Ocean Sea, as well as viceroy and governor of any territory he discovered, and be awarded 10 percent of any earnings made from his discovery. In return, King Ferdinand and Queen Isabella of Spain would gain lands plus 90 percent of the profits from his explorations. In 1497, John Cabot obtained a royal charter from King Henry VII of England to explore what would become known as North

America. Cabot was given a ship, supplies, and a crew, along with 80 percent of any profits made. King Henry would receive 20 percent of any profits and ownership of any new lands that were discovered.

In this simulation, students can decide to accept a charter either from Spain or Portugal. Both charters give any lands discovered to the country backing the expedition, but they vary in what they offer the explorers in exchange. Depending on the country, the ship, crew, maps and charts, and supplies it offers may be rated as either poor or good. Read more about the Royal Charters offered by Spain and Portugal—as well as how these charters will affect the simulation—on pages 24 and 25.

Conducting the Simulation

This simulation is divided into five episodes—one for each day of the school week—each re-creating the challenges and experiences of the early explorers as their ships sailed from western Europe to the Americas. Each episode should take about 45–60 minutes, depending on your class size. Consider starting the actual simulation on a Monday so that it will run its course by Friday. Complete all preparatory work (e.g., building background knowledge, forming groups, and choosing characters) during the previous week.

Each episode consists of two scenarios, which feature problem-solving activities that simulate some of the difficulties and experiences that the explorers faced. How well students negotiate these challenges will determine their success or failure as explorers of the "new world." At the end of the simulation, students will engage in a discussion and debriefing of the simulation experience.

A Sample Scenario

The scenario presented in each episode is where students actually get to participate in a historical event. Below is an abbreviated version of the first scenario in Episode 1 ("Following a Dream") to demonstrate how a simulation scenario might typically run.

Read or paraphrase the introduction to the episode, then describe the scene in which the explorers arrive at the royal court of Spain, where they are granted an audience with King Ferdinand and Queen Isabella. After reading the king and queen's offer (see Royal Charter of Spain, page 24), allow the explorers to discuss their next step. Then invite a spokesperson from each group to present the group's decision. (Choose a different spokesperson from each group every day.)

Teacher: Okay, has everyone had enough time to decide what they want to do? Great! Explorer Group 1, what did you decide?

Explorer Group 1 Spokesperson: We decided to take Spain's offer.

Teacher: All right. *(Noting on a piece of paper that Group 1 is taking Spain's offer)* Explorer Group 2?

Explorer Group 2 Spokesperson: Yeah, we'll do that, too.

Teacher: You want to take Spain's offer as well? Okay. *(Notes that down as well)* Group 3?

Explorer Group 3 Spokesperson: Is there any other country that might have a better deal for us?

Teacher: Who could you ask?

Explorer Group 3 Spokesperson: The king and queen?

Teacher: Sure.

Explorer Group 3 Spokesperson: Hey, is there another country that we can ask for a Royal Charter?

Teacher: *(Using his or her best Spanish aristocratic voice to get into character)* If you do not find our offer to your liking, then perhaps you can find someone in Portugal who will sponsor your little expedition!

Explorer Group 3 Spokesperson: *(After consulting with the rest of her group)* We're going to ask Portugal what they have to offer. Maybe we can get a better deal.

Teacher: Okay. *(Notes that Group 3 is going to ask Portugal)* Explorer Group 4?

Explorer Group 4 Spokesperson: We want to go to Portugal, as well.

Teacher: Sure. *(Noting down Group 4's decision)* Okay, Explorer Group 5, what do you want to do?

Explorer Group 5 Spokesperson: We like that idea. We want to go somewhere else, too.

Teacher: Fine. *(Notes down this decision)* Okay, everyone let's see what happens because of your decisions. *(Refers to the Royal Charter of Spain)* Explorer Groups 1 and 2, write down that you have been given a caravel type of ship. Decide what to name your ship and use this handout to start your ship's log. *(Hands the two groups the Royal Charter of Spain)* Explorer Groups 3, 4, and 5, you have traveled across the border to meet with King Manuel I of Portugal. Using your connections in the royal court of Portugal, you have managed to get an audience. After listening to your plans to sail to the New World, King Manuel offers you a ship and supplies and a share of whatever riches you may find on your travels. The ship offered by the king sounds better than the one offered by Spain, but the supplies are not nearly as good as you had hoped. So, are you going to take this offer or go back and try to take Spain's offer instead? Remember, you may have insulted King Ferdinand and Queen Isabella by not taking their offer the first time. . . .

This is how the scenarios will typically run, with role-playing students dealing with the situations that confront them, and you, the teacher, acting out all the other parts while coordinating the simulation. Present the situation in the scenario to students and then give them time to make their decisions. You have to stay on your toes because students may come up with a solution different from those offered in the simulation. In such cases, you can either wing it and accommodate them, or tell them that they must stick to the options offered in the simulation. Do not reveal the outcome of each student's or group's decision until everyone has weighed in; only then do you respond to each person or group, with the rest of the class observing the outcome of the choices as scripted in the scenario.

Embarking on the Journey

Three key factors will determine the success or failure of an expedition:

1. the condition of the ship's supplies

2. the ship's navigation

3. the crew's morale

Various conditions during the simulation can affect these factors. During the course of the simulation, students will be asked to make a variety of skill spins to determine the consequences of their choices. If the spin fails (a number higher than the skill number is spun), you will have to consult one of the following tables, and students will have to make another spin to determine the outcome of the first failed spin.

- Ship's Supplies Table (page 26)

- Disease Table (page 27)

- Navigation Table (page 28)

- Crew Morale Table (page 29)

- Ship's Mishap Table (page 30)

In addition, students must monitor the passage of time during the simulation. This will vary from ship to ship, so you may want to have a calendar handy to help you and your students keep track of how much time has passed for each expedition. For example, say all ships set sail on August 1, 1495, and travel for two weeks, but Ship 1 misses a Navigation spin. That group must now add two extra weeks to their voyage—a predicament that could affect their supplies and possibly the crew's morale.

Supplies

As was the case for explorers in the late 15th and early 16th centuries, one of the greatest challenges students will face is having enough food and water to make the journey. Columbus wrote in his log that they had loaded dried meat, salted fish, and some fruits onto the ships. The fruits were eaten first because they would soon spoil. Other typical fare included bacon, hard biscuits, cheese, oil, and salt. Sailors also fished during the journey to supplement their diets. Having enough fresh water was often a problem so explorers brought beer and wine because alcohol did not spoil as quickly as water.

At various intervals during the simulation, a Supply Check will be called for to determine the condition of the ship's supplies. The Ship's Steward is best suited for this job, but any explorer in the group can make this spin. **During a Supply Check, an explorer must spin a number equal to or lower than her Common Sense number to keep the supplies in good condition.** If the Supply Check fails (the number spun is higher than the explorer's Common Sense number), the ship's supplies are in jeopardy and a second spin must be made on the Ship's Supplies Table.

Navigation

Early explorers literally sailed into the unknown, with only the barest knowledge of the direction in which they should sail. Using simple tools such as a compass (used to find magnetic north), an hourglass (used in a method called "dead reckoning," in which a ship's speed was determined by counting how many knots in a rope were pulled off the ship by a floating log during a set period of time), and an astrolabe or back staff (used for celestial navigation to determine a ship's latitude), these brave sailors had to find their way safely across the Atlantic Ocean. Our simulation, however, is set in 1495, after Columbus had charted the way to the Americas. Because he had sailed for Spain, the Spanish have better maps and charts than the Portuguese.

For every week the expedition is at sea, explorers must make a Navigation Check, as called for in each scenario. (Explorers sailing for Portugal must add 1 to the number they spin during these checks to account for their poor maps and charts.) **During a Navigation Check, an explorer must spin a number equal to or lower than his**

Seamanship number to keep the ship on course. If the Navigation Check fails (the number spun is higher than the explorer's Seamanship number), a second spin must be made on the Navigation Table.

The Ship's Crew and Morale

Sailors during the Age of Discovery were a mixed lot. Some sailors were professional seamen who made their living as fishermen or merchant traders, while others were formally trained in sailing schools, such as the one established in Portugal by Prince Henry. Many either learned the trade from their fathers or left home and went to sea, as did a young Christopher Columbus, whose father was a weaver in Genoa, Italy. And still others were convicted criminals, even murderers, who were promised a pardon if they would sail with an explorer. On his first voyage across the Atlantic Ocean, Columbus sailed with a convicted murderer as part of his crew.

In this simulation, explorers have either a well-trained and experienced crew from Portugal or a mix of convicts and veteran seamen from Spain. At the beginning of the voyage, both crews start with a Morale of 5. This should be recorded in the Ship's Log kept by each group. Different situations can cause the crew's Morale to go up (but never higher than 5) or down, depending on how events occur.

When a Morale Check is called for, an explorer from each group should spin the spinner. If the number spun is higher than the crew's current Morale, the person must refer to the Crew Morale Table and make another spin. If the crew's Morale ever drops to 0, a spin on the Crew Morale Table is automatically made. Only after the spin results have been resolved can the crew's Morale be reset at 1.

Assessing and Evaluating

Throughout the unit students should be evaluated on their historical understanding. You can do this by assessing the authenticity and historical accuracy of the way they play their character and the log entries they've written throughout this simulation.

Use the rubrics on page 31 to give each student a daily score, based on the student's log entries and your observations. Each rubric is scored on a scale of 1 to 5, with 1 being the lowest possible score and 5 the highest. Add the two scores from Rubrics #1 and #2 to generate a number from 2 to 10. To convert this total score to a percentage score, multiply the total score by 10. You can award scores such as 4.5 if you feel a student was at least a 4 but not quite a 5. This daily percentage score can then be averaged over the week to generate an individual score for each student.

	Student Log		Teacher Observations		Score Percentage
Monday	3	+	4	× 10	70%
Tuesday	4	+	4	× 10	80%
Wednesday	3.5	+	5	× 10	85%
Thursday	2.5	+	4	× 10	65%
Friday	4	+	5	× 10	90%
Average for the week					78%

Another piece of the assessment puzzle is the group dynamic. This simulation is the perfect setting for teaching students the value of teamwork and collaboration. At the end of each day's simulation, as students are recording in their personal logs, debrief quickly with each group to discuss how they worked together as a group. Were they patient with one another? Were they respectful of one another's opinions? Did the group dynamic feel supportive or combative? Based on this discussion, use Rubric #3 to record a group score for that day.

At the end of the week, total the group score and then multiply by 4 in order to give the group a percentile score. After the simulation is finished, combine the group's scores with each member's daily scores to give each student a final grade for the simulation. For example, say one group's scores are as follows:

	Group's Daily Score
Monday	4
Tuesday	4
Wednesday	5
Thursday	3
Friday	5
Total	21 × 4 = 84%

A student with an individual score of 78% combined with his group score of 84% will get a final average score for the simulation of 81%, or a B.

The Life of an Explorer

In the late 1400s, people in Europe eagerly explored the world around them, searching for new and better ways to trade with people in other parts of the world, especially the Far East. Europeans yearned for the spices, jewels, perfumes, and silk cloth that could be found only in places like China and the East Indies.

To get to Asia, the Portuguese sailed around Africa, but the voyage was perilous and took a very long time. Christopher Columbus tried to find a shortcut to Asia by sailing west from Spain, but instead stumbled upon the Americas, a place that Europeans didn't even know existed. Thus, the "old world" of Europe met the "new world" of the Americas.

During this "Age of Discovery," the life of an explorer was both exciting and treacherous. Floating on a seemingly endless ocean aboard a small wooden ship, sailors feared that if they sailed too far from land they would fall off the edge of the earth. Several believed in giant sea monsters and mermaids. And yet for all their superstitious beliefs, religion played a big role in explorers' lives. A day on board a ship typically began with

Easy Simulations: Explorers © 2008 by Tim Bailey Scholastic Teaching Resources

prayer and ended with religious services. Then the sailors set to work in four-hour shifts, pumping seawater and filth out of the ship's bilge, cleaning and wetting the deck, working the sails, and checking lines and cargo. They slept on the hard wooden deck. (The Native Americans they later encountered taught them how to make and use hammocks.)

Meals were cooked on deck in a small firebox when the sea was calm and if someone had been lucky enough to catch a fish. Most meals, however, were eaten cold. Sailors often dined on tasteless hard biscuits (sometimes with weevils in them), oatmeal (also filled with bugs), bacon and dried meat, dried fruit, dried peas, cheese, and oil. Drinking water would go bad after several weeks at sea. Unless there was rainwater to refill the water barrels, sailors drank from a large store of beer and wine, which took longer to spoil. Many sailors died from either consuming spoiled supplies or not having enough to eat or drink.

Diseases were another problem for sailors. There were no antibiotics, vaccines, or any modern medicines so many explorers died of a variety of illnesses, such as dysentery, typhus, and scurvy. (The sailors would later spread fatal diseases, such as smallpox, to the Native Americans, wiping out whole populations who had no resistance to these European illnesses.)

There were many other challenges that these early explorers faced. A dead calm, in which no wind blew, would leave a sailing ship motionless on the ocean for days, while violent storms could tear a ship apart. Hunger and boredom could drive the crew to mutiny, and sharp underwater reefs could rip through the ship's bottom. Yet despite all of these dangers and difficulties, many explorers sailed into the unknown and brought back the knowledge of what waited beyond the horizon.

Name: _____   Date: _____

Choose a Role

Select the role that you would like to play during the explorer simulation.
Record your choice and your attributes in your personal log.

Roles	Strength	Common Sense	Seamanship	Negotiation Skill	Medical Expertise	Health
Navigator	2	4	5	2	2	5
Helmsman	4	3	5	1	2	5
Ship's Surgeon	2	4	1	3	5	5
Boatswain	3	3	3	5	1	5
Steward	3	5	2	3	2	5
Interpreter	2	3	1	5	4	5

Navigator – You are responsible for keeping the ship on course and not getting lost. You are skilled at using navigational tools, such as a compass, astrolabe, and back staff, and also proficient at reading maps and charts.

Helmsman – You are responsible for steering the ship as it sails on the ocean, following the course laid out by the navigator. You are very capable of handling the ship in storms and rough seas.

Ship's Surgeon – As the doctor on the ship, you can mean the difference between life and death if someone falls ill or is injured in an accident. Medicine in the late 15th and early 16th centuries was more folk wisdom than science, but it was usually better than nothing.

Boatswain – You are responsible for the ship's crew, making sure they follow the captain's orders and work hard. Because of your dealings with the captain and crew, you are very good at negotiating.

Steward – You are in charge of the ship's supplies, especially the food and water that the crew needs to survive. You fully understand that the crew may mutiny if you run out of good food and water.

Interpreter – As a scholar who has studied several languages, you will be relied on to communicate with whomever the explorers may encounter. You are an excellent negotiator and are skilled in medicine, having studied at a university.

Easy Simulations: Explorers © 2008 by Tim Bailey, Scholastic Teaching Resources

Personal Log

Explorer's Name: _____

Explorer's Role: _____

_____

Sailing for the Country of _____

On board the Good Ship _____

Explorer's Skills:

Strength: _____

Common Sense: _____

Seamanship: _____

Negotiation Skill: _____

Medical Expertise: _____

Health: _____

_____ Personal Log

Date _____

_____

_____

_____

_____

_____

_____

_____

_____

_____

_____

_____

_____

Name: _____   Date: _____

Ship's Log

Of the Good Ship _____

Sailing for the country of _____

Ship's Crew Members:

Name	Role
1. _____	_____
2. _____	_____
3. _____	_____
4. _____	_____
5. _____	_____

Royal Charter _____

Crew's Morale _____

For each category, circle one:

Ship	good	poor
Crew	good	poor
Supplies	good	poor
Maps	good	poor

Weeks Traveled (make a tally mark for each week you have traveled)

Royal Charter of Spain

Offer	Condition	Description
Ships	Poor	A caravel, a 64-foot-long ship with three triangular lateen sails, which makes the ship easy to handle but diminishes its speed on the open sea. It has a crew of 24 men. The ship is not as durable as the one offered by Portugal, however.
Supplies	Good	Spain fully supports the exploration of the New World and provides its explorers with ample supplies.
Maps and Charts	Good	Since Columbus had already traveled to the Americas under the flag of Spain in 1492—and this voyage is taking place in 1495—Spain already possesses up-to-date maps and charts for the journey across the Atlantic.
Crew	Poor	King Ferdinand and Queen Isabella provide you with a crew made up largely of convicts, who can gain a pardon by sailing with you. Only a few experienced sailors will join these crooked crewmen.

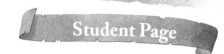

Royal Charter of Portugal

Offer	Condition	Description
Ships	Good	A caravela redonda, an 85-foot-long ship with two square sails and one triangular lateen sail. It has a crew of 32 men. Portugal is widely recognized as the master shipbuilder of this age. This is the most popular and seaworthy ship of the time.
Supplies	Poor	Portugal does not have much interest in going west to find Asia. They had already invested a great deal of time and money in finding a way to Asia by sailing around Africa. Therefore, the explorers are not given the best of supplies.
Maps and Charts	Poor	In 1494, Pope Alexander VI negotiated an agreement with Spain and Portugal that gave land and exploration rights in the New World to both countries. However, Portugal does not have the updated maps and charts that Spain does.
Crew	Good	Portugal is envied for the high quality of sailors and captains that sail for the king. Since the opening of Prince Henry the Navigator's school for seamen in the 1400s, many sailors from Portugal have been well trained.

Ship's Supplies Table

When a Supply Check is called for, an explorer from each group must spin his Common Sense number or lower to keep the ship's supplies in good condition. If the Supply Check fails (the number spun is higher than the explorer's Common Sense number), the ship's supplies are in jeopardy. Another spin must be made on the following table.

 NOTE: Explorers sailing for Portugal must add 1 to the number they spin during Supply Checks to account for their poor supplies.

If you spin . . .	Then . . .	Do this . . .
1	The water in the ship's barrels has a greenish scum on it and a peculiar smell. You can even see little white larvae floating in the water. The ship's water has gone bad and can cause illness.	To avoid disease, everyone must spin his Health number or lower. If a person fails in his spin, he must make a spin on the Disease Table.
2	The meat has a shiny green tint to it and smells sort of sweet. It is going rancid.	To avoid disease, everyone must spin their Health number or lower. If a person fails in her spin, she must make a spin on the Disease Table.
3	The hard biscuits are rock-hard, and little weevils are crawling in them.	Due to the poor quality of the food, lower the crew's Morale by 1 point. Make this adjustment in the Ship's Log. Poor food quality caused more mutinies than any other factor on board a ship!
4	The fishing has been extremely poor this week, and rations have been cut in half.	Lower the crew's Morale by 1 point in the Ship's Log.
5	Someone has been stealing from the ship's supplies, and now everyone on the crew is looking at one another suspiciously.	Lower the crew's Morale by 1 point in the Ship's Log.

6	The crew is weak and sleepy. Rations have been so poor all week that the crew is malnourished.	Lower everyone's Health by 1 point. Everyone must spin a number equal to or lower than their new Health number. If a person fails in his spin, he must make a spin on the Disease Table.
		
		  The crew is too weak to mutiny, so the Morale level stays the same.
		
		  Malnourishment was a very serious condition suffered by sailors, caused by lack of vitamins in the diet. It made the crew vulnerable to colds, flu, and other diseases.

Disease Table

Spin once on this table to determine the consequences of contracting a disease.

If you spin . . .	You have . . .	Do this . . .
1 or 2	**Dysentery** – a disease of the large intestine caused by an amoeba; sailors called this disease "the flux." You suffer from stomach cramps and diarrhea.	Subtract 1 Health point. To keep you from losing additional Health points, another explorer in your group must spin a number equal to or lower than his Medical Expertise number. If the spin fails, you lose 1 more Health point. Only one Medical Expertise spin can be attempted.
3 or 4	**Typhus** – contracted from body lice and other parasites. You get a high fever and muscle aches.	Subtract 1 Health point. To keep you from losing additional Health points, another explorer from your group must spin a number equal to or lower than her Medical Expertise number. If the spin fails, you become delirious and lose 1 more Health point. A different explorer can attempt another Medical Expertise spin. This continues until either the Medical Expertise spin succeeds or you die.
5 or 6	**Scurvy** – results from lack of vitamin C in the diet. Your gums are bleeding and your teeth have become loose and started to fall out. You feel weak and unable to work. (This condition led to the suffering and death of many early explorers.)	Subtract 1 Health point. For every week that you are at sea after developing this condition, you must make a Health spin. On each spin, you must spin your Health number or lower to keep from losing another Health point. This continues until you either die or reach the Americas, where you can eat some fresh fruits and vegetables.

Navigation Table

When a Navigation Check is called for, an explorer from each group must spin her Seamanship number or lower to keep the ship on course. If the Navigation Check fails (the number spun is higher than the explorer's Seamanship number), a second spin must be made on the table below.

NOTE: Explorers sailing for Portugal must add 1 to the number they spin during a Navigation Check to account for their poor maps and charts.

If you spin . . .	Then . . .	Do this . . .
1 or 2	The ship has gone off course.	Add one week to your journey and record this in your Ship's Log. Make another Supply and Navigation Check.
3 or 4	The ship's crew does not trust the Captain or the Navigator's reports about the reliability of the maps and charts.	Lower the crew's Morale by 1 point. Columbus kept two separate logs of his first voyage—one had the actual distance traveled and the other recorded a shorter distance traveled. Historians believe that he showed this second log to the crew so that they would not become discouraged by how far they had traveled without sighting land.
5 or 6	The ship is severely off course.	Add two weeks to your journey and record this in your Ship's Log. Make two extra Supply and Navigation Checks.

Easy Simulations: Explorers © 2008 by Tim Bailey, Scholastic Teaching Resources

Crew Morale Table

When a Morale Check is called for, an explorer from each group must spin the spinner.
If the number spun is higher than the crew's current Morale, refer to the following table.
If the crew's Morale drops to 0, a spin on this table must also be made.

If you spin . . .	Then . . .	Do this . . .
1	The crew threatens to stop working.	An explorer can try to negotiate with the crew by making a spin. If he spins his Negotiation Skill number or lower, the crew agrees to go back to work. If the spin fails, add one week to the journey and make another Supply and Navigation Check. The ship then proceeds as normal.
2	A fight breaks out among the crew, and a sailor is stabbed.	An explorer can try to help the stabbed sailor by making a Medical Expertise spin. If she spins her Medical Expertise number or lower, she saves the life of the sailor. If the spin fails, the sailor dies. Subtract 1 point from the crew's Morale. Spin again if the crew's Morale is already 0.
3	Careless sailors forget to store the food properly.	On the next Supply Check, add 1 to the number spun (to increase the difficulty level).
4	A crew member on duty does not turn the hourglass on time and causes an error on the distance recorded for that day's travel.	On the next Navigation Check, add 1 to the number spun (to increase the difficulty level).
5	Someone has sabotaged the ship!	Make a spin on the Ship's Mishap table.
6	The crew is very angry and is threatening mutiny!	Two explorers must try to negotiate with the crew by each making a Negotiation Skill spin. If both explorers spin their Negotiation Skill number or lower, they've succeeded in calming down the crew. If an explorer fails in his spin, he is attacked by an angry crew member. The explorer must spin his Strength number or lower to successfully defend himself. Otherwise, he must subtract 1 point from his Health number. In addition, add one week to the journey and make an additional Supply and Navigation Check because of the crews' uncooperative mood.

NOTE: When two or more spins are called for, spin again to avoid duplicated results.

Ship's Mishap Table

Spin on this table to see what damage the ship has incurred.

If you spin . . .	Then . . .	Do this . . .
1	The shrouds—the ropes that support the mast—have become tangled.	Two explorers must make Seamanship spins, spinning their Seamanship number or lower. If either one fails, add one week to the journey and make an additional Supply and Navigation Check.
2	One of the yardarms, which support the sail, has broken.	To replace the yardarm, an explorer must spin a number equal to or lower than her Seamanship number and her Strength number. If either spin fails, add one week to the journey and make an additional Supply and Navigation Check.
3	The mizzenmast—a large upright pole that has the sail rigged to it—has broken and is collapsing onto the deck.	Each explorer in the group must spin his Strength number or lower to avoid being hit by the mast. If anyone fails the spin, he loses 1 Health point. To restore the lost Health point, another explorer must spin her Medical Expertise number or lower. In addition, two Strength and two Seamanship spins must be made successfully by separate explorers to repair the ship. For each spin that fails, add one week to the journey and make additional Supply and Navigation Checks.
4	The firebox used for cooking has been overturned and has started a fire.	To quickly put out the fire, three explorers must spin their Common Sense number or lower. If anyone fails the spin, she is burned and loses 1 Health point. To restore the lost Health point, another explorer must spin his Medical Expertise number or lower. In addition, for every failed spin, add one week to the journey and make additional Supply and Navigation Checks.
5	The hatch on the hatchway has failed, and seawater has poured into the ship's supplies.	On the next Supply Check, add 1 to the number spun (to increase the difficulty level).
6	The rudder has broken.	An explorer must spin his Strength number or lower to dive overboard and try to fix the rudder. If the spin fails, he loses 1 Health point from being injured while trying to fix the rudder. To restore the lost Health point, another explorer must spin her Medical Expertise number or lower. Regardless of the outcome of the Strength spin, the explorer must now spin his Seamanship number or lower to successfully fix the rudder. The ship may then go on as normal. If the spin fails, add 1 to the number spun on every Navigation Check from now on (to increase the difficulty level).

NOTE: When two or more spins are called for, spin again to avoid duplicated results.

Easy Simulations: Explorers © 2008 by Tim Bailey, Scholastic Teaching Resources

RUBRIC #1
Student's Log

1 – Student did not record any events that occurred during the simulation.

2 – Student recorded very little about what occurred during the simulation.

3 – Student recorded information about what occurred during the simulation but in an incomplete fashion.

4 – Student recorded all of the important occurrences of the day's simulation, but not in a first-person narrative style.

5 – Student wrote detailed facts about the occurrences during the simulation and embellished these with personal thoughts in a believable first-person narrative style.

Score: _____

RUBRIC #2
Teacher Observations

1 – Student was disruptive and prevented others from being able to participate in the simulation.

2 – Student did not participate in group discussions or simulation activities. Student might have been argumentative or disrespectful to other members of the group.

3 – Student either monopolized the group discussions or participated at a minimal level.

4 – Student participated well in the activity and allowed others to participate as well.

5 – Student was gracious in his or her participation and encouraged others to become engaged as well. Student role-played parts of the simulation to the best of his or her abilities.

Score: _____

RUBRIC #3
Group Dynamics

1 – Very poor. Members were fighting, sullen, ineffective.

2 – Poor. Members were arguing and generally ineffective, although they may have accomplished some of the simulation's tasks.

3 – Adequate. No real arguing or put downs of group members but not very supportive of one another. The simulation's tasks were completed by the group.

4 – Good. Effective use of group time and good support of group members.

5 – Great. Fantastic group participation as well as support from group members of one another. Group members all felt free to participate and contribute their ideas.

Score: _____

Total Score: _____

Simulation Spinner

DIRECTIONS:

Use this spinner at various points during the simulation to determine the outcome of a situation.

Using the Spinner

To make a pointer, place one end of a paper clip over the center of the spinner.
Place a pencil on the center and spin the paper clip around the pencil point.

Episode 1

Following a Dream

OVERVIEW

Explorers seek audience with the monarchs of Spain and/or Portugal to ask for a Royal Charter that would enable them to sail to the "new world."

When students have gathered with their explorer groups, read aloud the following passage:

June 1495

You have always dreamed of traveling to far-off lands and finding rare and valuable treasures, and then returning home to fame and glory. Now those dreams seem within reach as you stand waiting in the blazing hot palace courtyard of King Ferdinand and Queen Isabella of Spain. You hope that they will give your group a Royal Charter that will enable you to sail west to the "new world" that Christopher Columbus was rumored to have discovered. But you are also aware that if the deal they offer is not to your liking, you can always go across the border to Portugal and ask King Manuel I for a Royal Charter from his country. You've heard that it took six years for Christopher Columbus to convince the King and Queen of Spain to giving him a Royal Charter. Hopefully, it won't take them that long to give you a favorable response.

Finally, a page steps into the courtyard and announces that the king and queen will see your group. As your eyes adjust to the dimly lit audience chamber, you see a man and a woman seated at one end of the large room, each one dressed in the finest clothes, embroidered in gold thread and set with jewels.

(continued)

Sounding more confident than you actually feel, you ask the king and queen to give you a Royal Charter and express your hope that they will grant your request. After a brief pause, the king replies, "No." King Ferdinand explains that they have already made a deal with Columbus, and as far as he knows no great riches have been brought from the lands that Columbus has discovered.

Downcast, you turn to leave, thinking you'll try your luck in Portugal. But then Queen Isabella speaks up. "I do not see any harm in letting you new explorers try your luck," she says. "Perhaps you will find the treasures that Columbus did not. And if these lands are not China but a 'new world,' as some are saying, then the people there can be converted to our religion, and the new world can be claimed as Spanish land." King Ferdinand reluctantly agrees and presents you with a Royal Charter.

The charter states that you will be given a caravel ship, an adequate vessel. (You were hoping for a better one.) Worse, they will give you a crew that is made up of only a few experienced sailors; the rest are convicts who will have their prison sentences erased if they will travel with you. On the bright side, the supplies of food and water look very good. In addition, because of Columbus's earlier voyages, you will have excellent maps and charts of the ocean. The Spanish monarchs are also offering 10 percent of any wealth that you may find and governorship of any lands that you may discover. This is about the same deal that Don Cristóbal Colón (Christopher Columbus) received in the Santa Fe Capitulations from King Ferdinand and Queen Isabella in 1492.

Inform the explorers that they must now decide if they will take this deal or try their luck with Portugal. Allow explorers to discuss their options within their groups. Then invite a spokesperson from each group to tell you their decision and record it on a piece of paper.

After all of the explorer groups have made their decision, give the groups that accepted Spain's Royal Charter a copy of the charter for their Ship's Log. If any group decided to go to the King of Portugal for a Royal Charter, read them the following passage:

You have traveled for days to reach the court of King Manuel I of Portugal. He must be in a generous mood because he agreed to see your group immediately without the usual wait of several weeks to months. After you have laid out your plans to sail west across the Atlantic Ocean, King Manuel replies that the king before him had turned down that Italian sailor Columbus years ago. And now it turns out that he actually found something for Spain! The king explains that Portugal and Spain have been rivals for many years but now have agreed to split up the lands found in this "new world."

To keep up with Spain, King Manuel offers you a Royal Charter but explains that he has had to cut some corners because Portugal still believes in reaching Asia by sailing around Africa. (Vasco da Gama will finally accomplish this for Portugal in 1498.) The Royal Charter of Portugal offers a *caravela redonda*, an excellent ship, and a crew of well-trained Portuguese sailors. However, the supplies that they are providing are not the best quality, and since none of their sailors have sailed that far west across the Atlantic Ocean, they have only the simplest of charts and maps. In addition, your group will receive 25 percent of all treasure found but you cannot claim any land or titles for yourselves.

Tell the explorers that they must now decide whether or not they are going to accept Portugal's deal. Allow explorers to discuss their options within their groups. Then invite a spokesperson from each group to tell you their decision and record it on a piece of paper. After you have heard everyone's decision, give the groups that accepted Portugal's Royal Charter a copy of the charter for their Ship's Log.

If any group decides not to take the deal, they must go back to Spain and beg King Ferdinand and Queen Isabella for another chance. Have the group choose someone with good Negotiation Skill to spin the spinner.

- If the person spins a number equal to or lower than his Negotiation Skill number, the group gets the original deal with Spain.

- If the spin fails (the person spins a number higher than his Negotiation Skill number), the group gets the same deal as before, except now they get the same poor supplies as are given to those sailing for Portugal.

After each group has worked out which country they will be sailing for, have the explorers record this information on their Personal Logs as well as their Ship's Log.

Episode 2

The Journey Begins

OVERVIEW

During this episode, explorers will be setting off on their voyage across the Atlantic Ocean. If they are sailing for Spain, they will be setting out from the port of Palo, Spain, on the morning of August 1, 1495. If they are sailing for Portugal, they will be leaving the port city of Lisbon on that same day.

Gather students together and read aloud the following description before they embark on their journey:

IN THEIR OWN WORDS . . .

"Friday, August 3, 1492. Set sail from the bar of Saltes at 8 o'clock, and proceeded with a strong breeze til sunset, . . . fifteen leagues south, afterwards southwest and south by west, which is the direction of the Canaries."

—Christopher Columbus, in his log as he began his journey

August 1, 1495

A warm breeze blowing this fine morning carries the salty smell of the ocean. You can hear the sound of a church bell in town as the crew loads the last of the ship's supplies. The Captain stands on the deck to see that everything is in order and then calls for the crew to make ready to sail. As you step on board, the smell of the ocean is replaced by the odor of the hot, sticky tar used to waterproof the ship, and the sound of the church bell is drowned out by a sharp crack as the wind fills the sails of your ship. As the ship turns toward the mouth of the harbor and the open sea, you look back to see friends and family waving good-bye. You can't help but wonder if you will ever see them again.

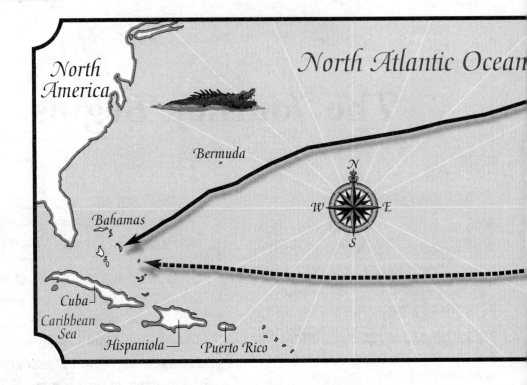

SCENARIO 1: THE FIRST STEP

Have explorers join their respective groups, then read aloud the following passage:

You have been traveling in known waters for a week and must now make a Supply Check and a Navigation Check. Since these waters are well mapped and the supplies are still fresh, subtract 1 from the number spun on each check.

For example, say your group is sailing for Spain and you choose your Helmsman to make the Navigation Check. Her Seamanship number is 5 and she spins a 6 (the highest number on the spinner). Subtracting 1 from this number results in a 5, which is equal to her Seamanship number. That means the Navigation Check is successful.

Remember: If your group is sailing for Portugal, you must add 1 to both Supply and Navigation Checks. That means that the number a Portuguese explorer spins will not be adjusted (–1 + 1 = 0). So a Portuguese Helmsman (with a Seamanship of 5) who spins a 6 will fail the Navigation Check and will have to spin on the Navigation Table.

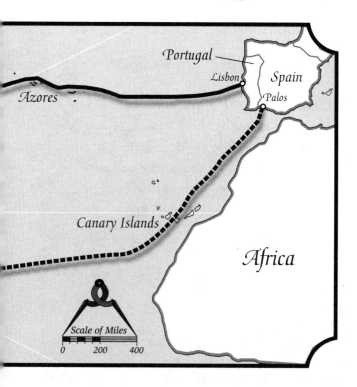

Give each group time to make their Supply and Navigation Checks (see pages 26 and 28).

After all the groups have resolved their Supply and Navigation Checks, tell them that they've now reached their first destination—the Canary Islands if they are sailing for Spain, or the Azores if they are sailing for Portugal. On these islands, explorers can refresh their supplies before sailing west.

Each group must now decide if the crew should be given shore leave before setting off again. Play the role of the Captain as you explain their options: *"If we do not give the crew shore leave and a chance to relax before we sail, we may have some very upset sailors. On the other hand, if we do give them shore leave, they may get into trouble on the island or even desert and not come back to the ship!"*

Allow explorers to discuss their options within their groups. Then invite a spokesperson from each group to tell you their decision, making note of it on a piece of paper. After all the groups have made their decision, read them the following results:

1. If you decide not to let the crew have shore leave, lower the crew's Morale by 1 point in the Ship's Log.

2. If you decide to let the crew have shore leave, explorers in your group will have to make Common Sense spins to keep the crew out of trouble.

   - If you have a good crew (from Portugal), make two Common Sense spins.

   - If you have a poor crew (from Spain), make three Common Sense spins.

Each spin must be made by a different explorer from the group. For each failed spin (an explorer spins a number higher than his Common Sense number), lower the crew's Morale by 1 point and add one week in the Ship's Log. (Additional Supply and Navigation Checks are not required for these weeks since they are spent in port trying to round up missing sailors.)

SCENARIO 2: BARELY A BREEZE

Inform students that their ship has been sailing due west for a week under a merciless sun and over seemingly endless seas. The decks are frequently wetted down with seawater to keep the wood from splitting under the heat of the sun.

Give each group time to make their Supply and Navigation Checks. After all the groups have resolved both checks, tell them that it is time to face their next challenge. Read aloud the following passage:

The sea looks as smooth as blue glass as the wind dies and the sails fall limp. The rolling of the ocean is the only movement of your vessel. The ship has hit a dead calm, and there is barely a breeze to be felt. After a couple of days without any wind, the Captain asks for your advice. He says, *"We have two choices: One, we can wait a while longer and see if the wind picks up again. Two, we can have some of the men go out in the ship's boat and try towing us until the wind picks up again."*

Allow explorers to discuss their options within their groups. Then invite a spokesperson from each group to tell you their decision, making note of it on a piece of paper. After all the groups have made their decision, read them the following results:

1. If you decide to wait for the wind to pick up again, choose someone from your group to spin on the following table:

Waiting for the Wind

If you spin . . .	Then . . .
1 or 2	The wind picks up, and the voyage continues.
3 or 4	Add one week to your travel time and make a Supply Check. The voyage continues.
5 or 6	Add one week to your travel time and make a Supply Check. In addition, choose someone from your group to make a Negotiation Skill spin because the crew is getting restless. • If the person spins her Negotiation Skill number or lower, the spin is successful and the crew stays calm. • If the spin fails, make a Crew Morale Check. If the number spun is higher than the crew's current Morale, refer to the Crew Morale Table to spin again and determine the consequences. After all these checks have been resolved, the voyage continues.

2. If you decide to have crew members tow the ship, choose two explorers from your group to make Negotiation Skill spins so they can talk the crew into doing such a difficult task.

    • If both explorers spin their Negotiation Skill number or lower, spin on the "Waiting for the Wind" table above, but subtract 2 from the number spun (if that number is 3 or higher).

    • If one or both Negotiation Skill spins fail, a Crew Morale Check must be made for each missed spin. When the Crew Morale Check has been resolved, spin on the "Waiting for the Wind" table, but subtract 1 from the number spun (if that number is 2 or higher).

Episode 3

Across the Sea of Darkness

OVERVIEW

Explorers ride through a terrible storm and could suffer severe losses if they get caught unprepared. After another week of sailing without sighting land, they must try to calm the troubled crew to keep them from turning against the captain.

SCENARIO 1: IT WAS A DARK AND STORMY NIGHT . . .

Have explorers join their respective groups, then read aloud the following passage:

You have spent another week at sea and must now make another Supply Check and Navigation Check. The Captain reports that the ship is making about 70 to 80 miles a day. However, you are sure that you are traveling at least 90 if not 100 miles per day. Why would the Captain lie to you?

IN THEIR OWN WORDS . . .

"Sunday, 9 September. Sailed this day nineteen leagues, and determined to count less than the true number, the crew might not be dismayed if the voyage should prove long."

—Christopher Columbus's log

Give each group time to make their Supply and Navigation Checks. After all the groups have resolved both checks, read aloud the following passage:

Tonight is particularly dark as heavy clouds screen the moon from sight. The sea grows rough, and a fine spray blows across the deck. Soon the wind begins to howl, and the sea spray stings your face and arms like needles. The deck begins to pitch, and you struggle to stay on your feet without being thrown to the deck or overboard into the cold, black water. The sails will be torn to shreds if they are not furled, and worse, if they are not taken down the ship could be capsized by the combination of wind and waves!

Instruct every explorer in each group to make a Common Sense spin then read the following consequences.

- If half or more of your group spin their Common Sense number or lower, you realize that a storm is coming and batten down the ship to prepare it for rough weather. Choose two explorers from your group to each make a Seamanship spin.

  ➡ If both explorers spin their Seamanship number or lower, you have skillfully ridden out the storm.

  ➡ If either spin fails, spin once on the Ship's Mishap Table (page 30).

- If fewer than half of your group spin their Common Sense number or lower, you are caught off-guard by the storm. Choose three explorers from your group to make Common Sense spins as they try to stay safe during the storm.

  ➡ If an explorer spins her Common Sense number or lower, she manages to avoid any mishaps during the storm.

  ➡ If an explorer fails his Common Sense spin (spins a number higher than his Common Sense number), he must make a Strength spin to determine if he holds on or is thrown overboard! If he fails his Strength spin, he is tossed into the water and immediately loses 1 Health point. Each explorer who is still on the ship can make a Strength spin to try and rescue the drowning person.

- If a person spins her Strength number or lower, she has successfully saved the explorer in the water. After the explorer has been rescued, another person in the group can make a Medical Expertise spin to try to restore 1 (and only 1) Health point lost by the unfortunate explorer.

- For every person who tries and fails her Strength spin, the person in the water loses an additional Health point. This continues until either everyone left on board has tried to rescue the person or the person has run out of Health points and has drowned.

In addition, your group must also choose two explorers to each make a Seamanship spin.

→ If both explorers spin their Seamanship number or lower, spin once on the Ship's Mishap Table to see what kind of damage your ship sustained from being unprepared.

→ If either spin fails, spin on the Ship's Mishap Table for every failed Seamanship spin. This means you could be spinning on the Ship's Mishap Table two times!

After the events above have been resolved, bring the class back together and read aloud the following passage:

Finally, by dawn, the wind has died down from a screaming gale to a steady breeze. The clouds begin to break up, and the white caps on the ocean calm. It is time to inspect your ship and see what kind of shape she is in.

Choose one person from your group to spin on the Storm Damage table (page 45). If your ship is rated as "good" (from Portugal), subtract 1 from the number you spin (if the number is 2 or higher).

Invite a representative from each group to come up and spin on the table below.

Storm Damage

If you spin . . .	Then . . .
1 or 2	Your ship sustained no damage. Your voyage continues uninterrupted.
3 or 4	Your sails have torn. Choose two explorers from your group to each make a Seamanship spin. • If both persons spin their Seamanship number or lower, you were able to repair the sails immediately and continue on your voyage. • If either spin fails, you lose one week of travel time. Make an extra Supply Check and Navigation Check.
5 or 6	Your mast has broken. Choose three explorers from your group to each make a Seamanship spin. • If all three persons spin their Seamanship number or lower, you were able to repair the mast immediately and continue on your voyage. • If any of the spins fail, you lose one week of travel time. Make an extra Supply Check and Navigation Check.

SCENARIO 2: CRAMPED, BORED, AND WEARING ON EACH OTHER'S NERVES

Inform students that another week at sea has passed, and they need to make another Supply Check and Navigation Check. After all the groups have resolved both checks, tell them that the crew is growing restless and worried. Read aloud the following passage:

"Why are we not there yet?" you hear the crew asking one another. To make matters worse the living conditions on the ship are getting pretty miserable. The ship reeks of too many people living too close together. When the crew is not on duty, they occupy their time by singing, gambling, or engaging in the latest sports—cockroach fights and rat hunting!

You overhear a group of sailors talking: "The Captain is a mad man! We must turn back or we will all be lost at sea forever!" It is up to you to calm down the crew and talk them into trusting the Captain for a while longer.

IN THEIR OWN WORDS . . .

"The [ship's] dwellings are so closed-in, dark, and evil smelling that they seem more like burial vaults. . . . For game in the neighborhood, there are fine fights of cockroaches — and very good rat-hunting, the rats so fierce that when they are cornered they turn on the hunters like wild boars."

—From the journal of Salazar, a 16th-century sailor

Each group must now choose two explorers to make Negotiation Skill spins in order to calm the crew.

- If both persons spin their Negotiation Skill number or lower, they have succeeded in convincing the crew to wait a while longer before taking matters into their own hands.

- If either spin fails, lower the crew's Morale by 1 point. A Crew Morale Check must be made.

Episode 4

Land Ho!

OVERVIEW

After sailing for several weeks, explorers finally catch sight of land and rejoice in their discovery. As they get ready to explore the New World, they meet some of the natives. Will they have a friendly encounter or a deadly one?

SCENARIO 1: A SIGN OF HOPE

Inform students that another week has passed and the crew has reached their breaking point. Give each group time to make their Supply and Navigation Checks. After all the groups have resolved both checks, read aloud the following passage:

Some of the crew is now openly hostile toward the Captain and those who support him. The Captain has declared that he will make an example of any sailor who tries to defy his orders. Whispers of mutiny can be heard from the most dissatisfied of the crew. You must try to reason with the Captain so he would not do anything rash. Otherwise, the situation on the ship could explode into violence.

IT'S A FACT!

In the winter of 1520, Ferdinand Magellan executed an officer who threatened mutiny during Magellan's famous voyage to circumnavigate the globe.

To reason with the Captain, each group must choose two explorers to make Negotiation Skill spins.

- If both people spin their Negotiation Skill number or lower, they have succeeded in calming the Captain, and the voyage continues as normal.

- If either spin fails, the Captain has one of the crew flogged for insubordination. Lower the crew's Morale by 1 point and make a Morale Check.

Continue reading:

Fortunately something happens to raise everyone's spirits. A bird is seen circling the ship's mast! Land cannot be too far away. Soon other signs of land are seen. A piece of driftwood is pulled onto the ship, and on it are fresh green leaves and red berries. It could not have been in the water too long. The crew is overjoyed at the signs of an end to this voyage. Raise your crew's Morale by 1 point.

The Captain has ordered extra hands on lookout and has offered a reward of 10,000 *maravedis* (equal to about $1,000 today) to the sailor who spots land first! (An experienced sailor of that time earned about 1,000 *maravedis* a month.)

In Their Own Words . . .

"Thursday, 11 October. Steered west-southwest . . . Saw pardelas and a green rush near the vessel . . . The crew of the *Niña* saw other signs of land, and a stalk loaded with rose berries. These signs encouraged them, and they all grew cheerful. Sailed this day till sunset, twenty-seven leagues."

—Christopher Columbus's log

To determine who spots land first, every explorer in each group must make a Seamanship spin.

- If only one person in the group spins her Seamanship number or lower, she receives the reward.

- If more than one person make a successful Seamanship spin, everyone who had a successful spin must spin again. The person who spins the highest number is the one who sighted land first and receives the reward.

Continue reading:

Hardly anyone on board the ship can sleep as they wait for a sighting of land. Suddenly in the gray light of predawn, a sharp cry is heard: "Land ho!" The crew rushes to the side of the ship where the lookout is pointing, and there it is—a dark shape outlined against the dark gray sky—land!

The crew must now wait until it is light enough to sail closer and then launch the ship's boat. Raise the crew's Morale by 1 point.

IN THEIR OWN WORDS . . .

"At two o'clock in the morning the land was discovered, at two leagues' distance . . . "

—Christopher Columbus's log

IN THEIR OWN WORDS . . .

" . . . the Admiral directed them to keep a strict watch upon the forecastle and look diligently for land, and to him who should first discover it he promised a silken jacket, besides the reward which the King and Queen had offered, which was an annuity of ten thousand maravedis."

—Christopher Columbus's log

Scenario 2: East Meets West

Read aloud the following passage:

As the sun slowly rises over the horizon, your ship sails in closer to what now appears to be an island. The Captain orders the ship's boat to be lowered over the side and you join him, rowing to shore on the gentle surf. When you near the shore, you jump over the side into the warm water and pull the boat up onto the sandy beach. You marvel at how good it feels to have solid ground under your feet again after so long at sea.

In Their Own Words . . .

"The Admiral called upon the two Captains, and the rest of the crew who landed, as also to Rodrigo de Escovedo notary of the fleet, and Rodrigo Sanchez, of Segovia, to bear witness that he before all others took possession (as in fact he did) of that island for the King and Queen his sovereigns . . ."

—Christopher Columbus's log

The Captain actually falls to the ground and kisses the land. You can see his face fill with emotion as he calls for the flags that you have brought from the ship. The Captain then plants the nation's flag into the white sand and calls on you to bear witness as he claims this land for the king.

As you look around, you see a lush, green forest with a crystal-clear stream running out from under the trees into the ocean. You notice what looks like ripe fruit and bright berries in the dense foliage. Your mouth starts to water at the prospect of fresh, cold water and a juicy piece of fruit. Suddenly you spot something moving in the brush. As you look closer you see several eyes looking back at you! What should you do?

1. Get out your weapons in case the natives are hostile.

2. Try to talk to whomever is in the forest.

3. Ignore the natives and see what they do.

Allow explorers to discuss their options within their groups. Then invite a spokesperson from each group to tell you their decision, making sure to take note of it on a piece of paper. After all the groups have made their decision, read them the following results:

IN THEIR OWN WORDS . . .

"Arrived on shore, they saw trees very green, many streams of water, and diverse sorts of fruits."

—Christopher Columbus's log

1. As you slide your swords from their scabbards and your knives from your belts, most of the natives run away. But a few brave ones come out of the forest and look at you curiously. One even steps forward and grabs a sword by the blade! He cries out as blood drips into the sand. Choose an explorer from your group to make a Medical Expertise spin to bandage the wounded native.

- If the person spins his Medical Expertise number or lower, he succeeds and the native smiles gratefully. The native offers the explorer a necklace with a polished shark's tooth.

- If the person spins a number higher than his Medical Expertise number, the native jerks his hand back and runs into the forest. No other natives will approach the group.

2. If you decide to try to talk to the natives, choose an explorer to make a Negotiation Skill spin. (If you choose an Interpreter to make the spin, subtract 1 from the number spun.)

- If the person spins her Negotiation Skill number or lower, the natives come out onto the beach. You learn that these people call themselves "Taino."

- If the person spins a number higher than her Negotiation Skill number, the natives look at you fearfully until one of the young men steps out of the trees and stands before you.

3. If you ignore the natives to see what they will do, the natives slowly come out from hiding. More people emerge from the forest, and soon a large group of natives is standing before you.

Continue reading:

As the natives come out onto the beach they approach cautiously. The people coming toward you have dark, straight hair and dark eyes. They have brown skin, and they wear decorative white or red paint on their nearly naked bodies. However, they seem to be friendly. Decide what to do next:

1. Try to trade beads and other trinkets with the natives.

2. Try to get them to tell you if there is gold or gems nearby.

3. Invite them to come on board the ship.

Allow explorers to discuss their options within their groups. Then invite a spokesperson from each group to tell you their decision, making sure to take note of it on a piece of paper. After all the groups have made their decision, read them the following results:

1. To trade with the natives, choose someone from your group to make a Negotiation Skill spin.

   - If the person spins his Negotiation Skill number or lower, the natives give you several hammocks, a couple of bright, feathered parrots, and a necklace with a gold nugget hanging from it. The Captain's eyes light up at this! Raise the crew's Morale by 1 point.

   - If the person spins a number higher than his Negotiation Skill number, the natives grow nervous and retreat into the forest.

2. To get information about gold and precious gems, choose two explorers from your group to make Negotiation Skill spins.

   - If both persons spin their Negotiation Skill number or lower, the natives communicate that a large island to the north has much gold and many gems. Raise the crew's Morale by 1 point.

   - If either Negotiation Skill spin fails, the natives do not offer any useful information.

IN THEIR OWN WORDS . . .

"They tell me of another island greater than the aforesaid Hispaña, whose inhabitants are without hair, and which abounds in gold above all others."
—Christopher Columbus's log

3. If you decide to invite the natives on board the ship, choose someone in your group to make a Negotiation Skill spin to help the natives overcome their fear and take your offer.

- If the person spins her Negotiation Skill number or lower, a great number of natives are soon swimming out to your ship and paddling toward it in dugout canoes. They bring many gifts, such as fishbone spears, parrots, colorful feather hats, and food that you have never seen before—big orange balls with green stems (pumpkins), slender vegetables from which they strip the little yellow pieces to eat (corn), and large, round, red fruits that are not sweet but very juicy (tomatoes). Raise the crew's Morale by 1 point.

- If the person spins a number higher than her Negotiation Skill number, the natives hold back and fearfully refuse to come to your ship.

IN THEIR OWN WORDS . . .

" . . . they came swimming to the boats, bringing parrots, balls of cotton thread, javelins, and many other things . . . "

—Christopher Columbus's log

IT'S A FACT!

Pumpkins, corn, and tomatoes are native to the Americas and were not known in Europe until explorers brought them home from the New World.

The Captain has decided it is now time to leave this beautiful island to seek the gold and precious gems that must be somewhere nearby. To ensure that the way to the islands with the most gold is found, the Captain has ordered that a number of natives—whom he calls "Indians" because he believes that you landed near the coast of India—be captured and taken to the ship to serve as guides.

IN THEIR OWN WORDS . . .

"I seized by force several Indians on the first island, in order that they might learn from us, and in like manner tell us about those things in these lands of which they themselves had knowledge . . . "

—Christopher Columbus's log

Glory, Greed, and Home!

OVERVIEW

In their search for riches, explorers run into some problems with the crew and with the ship. After a few hardships, they get ready to sail back home.

SCENARIO 1: IN SEARCH OF GOLD

Have explorers join their respective groups, then read aloud the following passage:

> You have been sailing around these islands for three weeks now. (Add this time to your logs, but no Supply or Navigation Checks are necessary.) The search for gold has been largely unsuccessful. One native chief had given the Captain a mask hammered from gold and set with beautiful stones. The Captain was so excited you thought he might have a heart attack! But when no more gold could be found in the chief's nearby village, the Captain flew into a rage and insisted that the natives were hiding the gold. Tension is rising among the crew. Some crew members are just as frustrated as the Captain because they thought this voyage would make them rich. But others believe that you should just take what you have and go home. Lower the crew's Morale by 1 point. Decide: Should you keep looking for gold or should you start the long voyage home?
>
> 1. Keep looking for gold.
> 2. Sail home now.

Allow explorers to discuss their options within their groups. Then invite a spokesperson from each group to tell you their decision, recording it on a piece of paper. After all the groups have made their decision, read them the following results:

1. If you decide to keep looking for gold, add one week to your Ship's Log. But you do not have to make Supply or Navigation Checks. The ship can resupply from the islands, and navigation is not a worry. However, the ship is sailing close to some unknown islands in uncharted waters.

    As the sun begins to set you see a swirling in the water just ahead. Choose two explorers from your group to make Common Sense spins.

    • If both explorers spin their Common Sense number or lower, they realize that what you are seeing is an underwater reef and that the ship is heading straight for it! They shout out a warning. Now another explorer must make two successful Seamanship spins in a row to safely steer the ship past the dangerous reef. If either of the Seamanship spins fails, the ship has struck the reef and you must spin on the "Underwater Reef" table below.

    • If either person spins a number higher than his Common Sense number, spin on the "Underwater Reef" table below.

Underwater Reef

If you spin . . .	Then . . .	Do this . . .
1 or 2	A groaning and horrible scraping sound is heard as the ship collides with the reef. Fortunately, a wave lifts the ship off the jagged coral and the ship is free again.	Choose an explorer to make a Seamanship spin to stay clear of the reef. • If the person spins her Seamanship number or lower, the ship may sail on with only some minor damage. • If the Seamanship spin fails, another spin must be made on the Underwater Reef table.

(continued)

Underwater Reef (continued)

If you spin . . .	Then . . .	Do this . . .
3 or 4	The ship shudders as it strikes the reef.	Choose two explorers to each make a Seamanship spin. The first spin is to steer off of the reef and keep the ship from taking further damage. The second spin is to get the sail cut down so that the wind does not drive the ship further onto the reef. • If both persons spin their Seamanship number or lower, the ship breaks free from the reef. But you lose two weeks while repairs are made to the ship. • If either spin fails, see the results for a 5 or 6 spin below.
5 or 6	The ship slams into the coral reef. A deep groaning and loud snapping can be heard below deck. Crew members come rushing up from below deck, saying that the ship is taking on water fast!	Everyone in the group must make a successful Strength spin (spin their Strength number or lower) or lose 1 Health point from being knocked off their feet by the impact. A successful Medical Expertise spin by another explorer can restore the lost Health point. To save the ship, everyone must also make a Seamanship spin to cut down the sails and throw all extra weight overboard so that the tide might lift the ship off the reef before the bottom is completely torn out! • If two or more Seamanship spins are missed (the number spun is higher than the person's Seamanship number), the ship is lost. The crew must abandon ship and swim for shore. • If fewer than two spins fail, the ship lifts off the reef. Although the ship is taking on water, it does not look as though it will sink. However, you will need four weeks of repairs.

If an explorer group's ship has sunk, each person in the group must make two successful spins in order to survive until someone from Europe comes to rescue them. The first spin is a Strength spin to survive the sharks and successfully swim to the nearby island. The second spin is a Common Sense spin to get along with the native population until rescue arrives. If either spin fails (the explorer spins a number higher than her Strength or Common Sense number), that explorer has perished!

If your ship has survived the reef, even the Captain has decided that it is time to sail for home.

> ## It's a Fact!
>
> After the *Santa Maria* struck a reef and sank on December 25, 1492, Columbus left 40 men behind on an island. When he returned six months later all 40 men had been killed by the native population.

2. If you decide to sail home now instead of staying and looking for gold, you will have to convince the Captain and the crew that it is a good idea. Choose an explorer to make both a Common Sense spin and a Negotiation Skill spin.

   - If the explorer spins his Common Sense number or lower and his Negotiation Skill number or lower, he has convinced the crew that to keep looking for gold is a waste of time. The crew is now on your side and can help you reason with the Captain.

   - If either of the spins fails, the crew does not agree with your plan to sail home. You can still talk to the Captain, however. To convince the Captain to sail home, choose two explorers to make Negotiation Skill spins.

     ➡ If both explorers spin their Negotiation Skill number or lower, the Captain agrees to turn the ship and head for home. However, because the crew is against the idea of going home now, lower their Morale by 1 point.

     ➡ If either spin fails, go to the #1 option (starting on page 56).

Scenario 2: Sailing for Home

Read aloud the following passage:

The Captain has decided that it is time to turn the ship toward the rising sun and sail for home. The very sound of the word *home* makes your heart swell as you think of how wonderful it will feel to see your friends and families again. At the same time, however, you still remember how difficult the voyage was to get here. The journey back will be just as dangerous. Yet there is one big difference between the voyage here and the voyage home—you know that it can be done.

You have been so wrapped up in the business of putting out to sea again that a tearful sob nearby startles you. You look over to see one of the proud Taino Indians stretching his hands toward the receding beautiful islands, his home. The Captain has decided to take several of the natives back with you to prove that you have really been to the New World. He claims that he is doing it for the Tainos' own good as well, explaining that now they will learn civilized ways and civilized religion.

Inform explorers that the journey home has raised the crew's spirits. Even those who wanted to stay and look for gold are excited at the prospect of seeing home again. Raise the crew's Morale by 1 point.

To ensure a safe and uneventful voyage home, each group must make four successful Supply and Navigation Checks. Add one week to the journey for every failed check. Ships sailing for Portugal do not need to adjust their Navigation spins anymore since they now have charted the route across the Atlantic. By the same token, these explorers also do not need to adjust their Supply spins since they were able to load abundant supplies from the islands.

It's a Fact!

Columbus took six Native Americans with him on his return trip to Spain, but only four survived the voyage. Later the Spanish enslaved the native populations in the Caribbean. However, since the native populations were later decimated by disease and because of their constant rebellions, it became necessary to import slaves from Africa as a labor force.

Read aloud the following passage:

All your life you have wanted nothing more than to leave behind the "old world" and discover a "new world." But seeing the coastline of Europe on the horizon, you now feel overwhelmed with joy at the sight of your own land. As your ship makes its way into port you can see that the entire town has filled the docks to watch your ship's return. Children run along the shore, waving as your ship passes. As your ship finally makes its way to the dockside, you set foot once again on dry land, knowing that your experience has changed you forever.

Epilogue

Read aloud the following passage:

It has been several weeks since you returned from your voyage of exploration and discovery. People still stop you on the street to ask you about the wonderful and mysterious things that you saw. However, an urgent request has arrived from the same royal court that provided you with your charter. The king has asked that you write a letter to the Royal Geographer and Cartographer so that the story of your journey can be added to the court library. You have to not only describe what you saw when you reached the New World but to write about your journey across the Atlantic Ocean. In addition to the facts about your adventure, the king also wants to know your feelings and thoughts about exploration and sailing into the unknown. He explains that what you write today will become the history that students will be reading tomorrow.

The Spice Trade

Why was finding a new way to reach Asia so compelling to explorers? Why was the spice trade so vital as to be worth risking your life by sailing into the unknown? While spices are used today to add flavor to food, they were used to keep food fresh back in the 16th century, before refrigeration and chemical preservatives were invented. This simple experiment will help demonstrate why spices were so important and valuable.

Put three oranges in a large container where they can be placed in a row with about four inches between each one. (I use an old aquarium because it makes it easy for the students to observe and keeps out the fruit flies.) Stud the first orange in the row with cloves. Leave the oranges alone for a couple of weeks. At the end of two weeks, you will observe that the orange with cloves is not rotting, while the orange on the opposite end of the row is turning black. The orange in the middle is only rotting on the side that is facing away from the cloves!

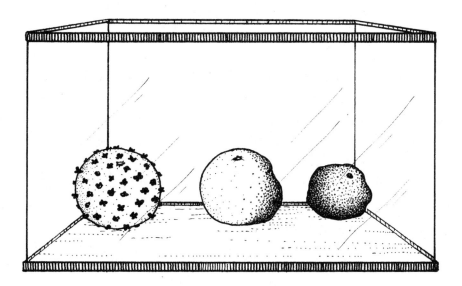

Navigation in the Age of Discovery: Astrolabe

In the early days of exploration, navigators used astrolabes to determine their distance north or south from the equator (their latitude) by looking at the position of the sun or a star, usually the North Star. Students can make their own astrolabes by following the instructions below.

To make an astrolabe, use a protractor or make your own out of cardboard. Tie one end of a foot-long piece of string to the middle of the protractor's crosspiece. On the other end of the string, tie a washer or a weight. Tape a drinking straw along the length of the crosspiece, as shown.

Using your astrolabe, sight the North Star through the straw and look at the degrees of angle your weighted string is crossing. This is your degrees of latitude. By taking a reading at the same time every night, a navigator could tell if his ship had moved nearer or farther from the equator and thus plot his course on a map.

Navigation in the Age of Discovery: Magnetic Compass

After his explorations in China, Marco Polo brought the concept of a compass to Europe. A compass always points to the magnetic north, so an explorer could use this information to determine what direction he is heading in. Invite students to make their own compasses by following the directions below.

Fill a shallow dish with water. Use a magnet to rub a needle repeatedly in one direction, from the eye to the pointed tip. This will align the molecules of the needle and magnetize it. Tape the needle to a small piece of Styrofoam and place it in the dish. The needle will spin to point to magnetic north. (If it does not work well then try to magnetize the needle with the magnet again.)

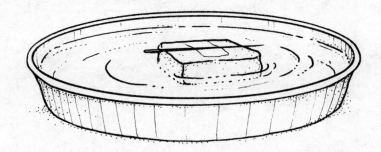

Resources

Books

If You Were There in 1492: Everyday Life in the Time of Columbus
by Barbara Brenner
(Aladdin, 1998)

The Picture History of Great Explorers
by Gillian Clements
(Frances Lincoln Children's Books, 2005)

Westward With Columbus
by John Dyson
(Madison Press Books, 1991)

Around the World in a Hundred Years
by Jean Fritz
(Putnam Juvenile, 1998)

Where Do You Think You're Going, Christopher Columbus?
by Jean Fritz
(Putnam Juvenile, 1997)

The History News: Explorers
by Michael Johnstone
(Candlewick, 1997)

You Wouldn't Want to Sail With Christopher Columbus! Uncharted Waters You'd Rather Not Cross
by Fiona Macdonald
(Franklin Watts, 2004)

The Discovery of the Americas: Prehistory Through the Age of Columbus
by Betsy Maestro
(HarperTrophy, 1992)

Exploration and Conquest: The Americas After Columbus: 1500–1620
by Betsy Maestro
(HarperTrophy, 1997)

Explorers Who Got Lost
by Diane Sansevere-Dreher
(Tor Books, 2005)

Encounter
by Jane Yolen
(Voyager Books, 1996)

Primary Sources Teaching Kit: Explorers
by Karen Baicker
(Scholastic, 2002)

Explorers: Literature-Based Activities for Thematic Teaching
by Glenda Nugent
(Creative Teaching Press, 1993)

Web Sites

The Columbus Navigation Homepage
http://www.columbusnavigation.com/

Explorers
http://edtech.kennesaw.edu/web/explorer.html

Kid Info: Explorers
http://www.kidinfo.com/American_History/Explorers.html

The Mariner's Museum: Age of Exploration
http://www.mariner.org/educationalad/ageofex/intro.php

Notes